COLORING WITH FAITH

(An adult coloring book with bible verses and religious affirmations)

Maria Montclair

How to use this coloring book

Meditate and reflect on the bible verses and affirmations as you color the illustrations.

33 beautiful mandalas will help you focus on your faith and the beauty of God's creations. Allow your mind to calm and relax while reaffirming your spirituality and beliefs.

Shut out the hectic world and the demands of modern life and find your inner peace with the Lord.

Join the millions of adults all around the world who are rediscovering the relaxation and joy of grown-up coloring! Share this special book with a friend—it makes a wonderful gift.

The fruit of the Spirit is love, joy, peace, patience, kindness, goodness, and faithfulness.

Come to me, all you who are weary and burdened, and I will give you rest.

Do not fear,
for I am with you.

Peace I leave with you;
my peace I give you.

We walk by faith,
not by sight.

Salvation is found in no one else but God.

Let the word of Christ dwell in you
richly in all wisdom.

Let your light so shine before men
that they may see your good works.

No man can serve two masters.

Do not be anxious about anything.

And the peace of God will guard
your heart and your mind.

Gentleness and self-control:
against such things there is no law.

Ask, and it shall be given.

God did not give us a spirit of timidity, but a spirit of power, of love and of self-discipline.

The Lord is good, a strong hold in the day of trouble.

Humble yourselves in the sight of the Lord,
and he shall lift you up

Walk in love.

Love your enemies.

For it is by grace you have been saved, through faith.

In all your ways acknowledge him,
and he shall direct your paths.

Faith is the substance of things hoped for,
the evidence of things not seen.

A merry heart does good like a medicine: but a broken spirit dries the bones

I can do all things through Christ.

Consider the ravens:
for they neither sow nor reap.

All have sinned and come short
of the glory of God.

God is faithful; he will not let you be tempted beyond what you can bear.

Weeping may endure for a night,
but joy comes in the morning.

We all are the work of your hand.

Love one another as I have loved you.

Delight yourself in the Lord; and he shall give you the desires of your heart.

Submit yourselves to God.

The Lord is my light
and my salvation.

Made in the USA
Middletown, DE
24 March 2016